Legends of the Elders

John W. Friesen
Illustrations by David J Friesen

Detselig Enterprises Ltd.

Calgary, Alberta, Canada

Legends of the Elders

© 2000 John W. Friesen

Canadian Cataloguing in Publication Data

Friesen, John W.

Legends of the elders

ISBN 1-55059-202-5

1. Indians of North America – Folklore. 2. Legends – North America. I. Title.

E98.F6F74   2000   398.2'089'97   C00-910335-X

Detselig Enterprises Ltd.

210-1220 Kensington Rd. N.W.

Calgary, Alberta   T2N 3P5

Telephone: (403) 283-0900

Fax: (403) 283-6947

e-mail: temeron@telusplanet.net

www.temerondetselig.com

We acknowledge the financial support of the Government of Canada through the Book Publishing Industry Development Program (BPIDP) for our publishing activities.

All rights reserved. No part of this book may be reproduced in any form or by any means without permission in writing from the publisher.

ISBN 1-55059-202-5

SAN 115-0324

Printed in Canada

Cover Design by Dean Macdonald & Alvin Choong.

Table of Contents

Introduction:
   The Significance of Indian Legends . 5

I. Entertainment Legends:
   Trickster Stories 9
   The Trickster and the Mice 11
   The Trickster and the Rock 13
   Napi and the Fruit 15
   Nanabush and the Birch Tree 19

II. Teaching Legends 21
   Why the Crow's Feathers are Black 23
   Why the Bear has a Short Tail 25
   A Special Talent 27
   How the Ghost River Got its Name 31
   The Origin of Maple Sugar 33
   The Origin of Lady Slippers 37

III. Moral Legends 39
   Strength in Unity 41
   Piah's Eagle Friends 43
   Wasted Talent 47
   Soar Like an Eagle 49
   The Gift Exchange 51
   A Story About Friends 55
   The Owl and the Goose 59
   Keeping Promises 61

To my grand-daughter, Victoria

happy reading, little one

Legends of the Elders

Introduction

The Significance of Indian Legends

Legends have sometimes been identified as the most common means of transmitting cultural values and beliefs. There was a time when all cultures relied solely on the oral tradition and there were no written forms of communication. Important belief systems, institutional rituals and cultural symbols were transmitted by the telling of legends or stories. Indian tribes specialized in the use of this medium.

Indian legends have a unique place in history. They are truly *Indian* stories, and as such they constitute the oral literature of each particular tribal cultural configuration. Indian stories are pictures of Indian life drawn by Indian artists, showing life from their point of view. Legends deal with religion, the origins of things and acts of bravery performed by stout-hearted warriors. They convey a vast range of cultural knowledge, including folkways, values and beliefs, and, in fact, often outline the very basis of a cultural pattern.

The study of Indian legends can be a very rich source of learning. Traditionally, legends appear to have been related for a variety of purposes and in at least two specific settings, formal and informal. The latter often took place at the spur of the moment when it appeared appropriate to reprimand or perhaps entertain someone. Also, sometimes on a winter evening, when tribesmen had stretched out to rest for the night, a storyteller would begin a tale. He would continue until it was evident that all of his hearers had fallen asleep. Formal storytelling was more directly connected to the occasion of deliberate moral or spiritual instruction. Some legends or myths were so sacred that their telling was restricted to the celebration of a very special event, such as the sundance. On these occasions, only recognized or designated persons could engage in their telling.

There appear to be at least four *kinds* of legends in use among North American Plains Indian tribes (with some degree of overlap), each of which has a special purpose. The four types of legends are:

Entertainment legends are often about the Trickster, who is called by different names among the various tribes. For example, the Blackfoot call him "Napi," the Crees call him "Wisakedjak," the Ojibway call him "Nanabush," the Stoneys call him "îktomni" and other tribes have different names for him. Stories about the Trickster are principally fictional and can be invented and amended even during the process of storytelling.

Trickster stories often involve playing tricks, that is, the Trickster plays tricks on others and they play tricks on him. The Trickster appears to have the advantage on his unsuspecting audience, however, since he possesses supernatural powers which he deploys on a whim to startle or to shock. He has powers to raise animals to life, and he may even die now and then and in four days come to life again. Aside from being amusing, Trickster stories often incorporate knowledge about aspects of Plains Indian culture – buffalo hunts, natural phenomena, rituals or the relationship between people and animals. In this sense these stories could also be categorized as instructional.

Instructional legends are basically employed for the purpose of dispensing information about the tribe's culture or history. These stories often utilize animal motifs to explain why things are the way they are. For example, a child may enquire about the origins of the seasons or creation, and a tale about animal life may be told. Sometimes these stories may include adventures of the Trickster.

7 Legends of the Elders

Moral legends are intended to teach ideal or "right" forms of behavior, and are employed to suggest to the hearer that a change in attitude or action would be desirable. Since traditional Indian tribes rarely corporally punished their children, they often found it useful to hint at the inappropriateness of undesirable behavior by telling stories. For example, the story might be about an animal who engaged in inappropriate behavior and the child was supposed to catch on that a possible modification of his or her own behavior was the object of the telling.

Sacred or spiritual legends can be related only by a recognized Elder or other approved individual and their telling is considered a form of worship. That tradition is respected in this volume.

In one tribe it was traditionally the custom that the services of an Elder had to be requested four days before the scheduled delivery of a sacred legend. The Elder in this case prepared for the event by fasting and offering gifts. Further, the legend could not simply be told at any time; the official period, when no payment was required, was the four days of winter solstice, "when the sun stands still." Other winter nights were permitted if the hearers would pay to hear the legend. Under no circumstances, however, could the legend, nor even any part of it, be told in the summer.

Spiritually significant stories were never told lightly to anyone who asked. Nor were they told by just anyone. In some tribes, sacred legends were considered property and thus their transmission from generation to generation was carefully safeguarded. Selected individuals would learn a legend by careful listening; then, on mastering the story, would pass it on to succeeding generations, perhaps changing aspects of the story to suit their own tastes. The amendments would centre on a different choice of animals or sites referred to in the story and preferred by the teller.

Legends comprised only a part of a tribe's spiritual system, which also included ceremonies, rituals, songs and dances. These were supplemented by physical objects such as fetishes, pipes, painted teepee designs, medicine bundles and shrines of sorts. Familiarity with these components comprised sacred knowledge, and everything learned was committed to memory. Viewed together, these entries represented spiritual connections between people and the universe which, with appropriate care, resulted in a lifestyle of assured food supply, physical well-being and the satisfying of the needs and wants of the society and its members.

One cannot overestimate the importance of Indian legends. Through this means would-be students of Aboriginal ways can learn a great deal about Indian philosophy and, hopefully, increase respect for their ways.

Entertainment Legends

10 *Legends of the Elders*

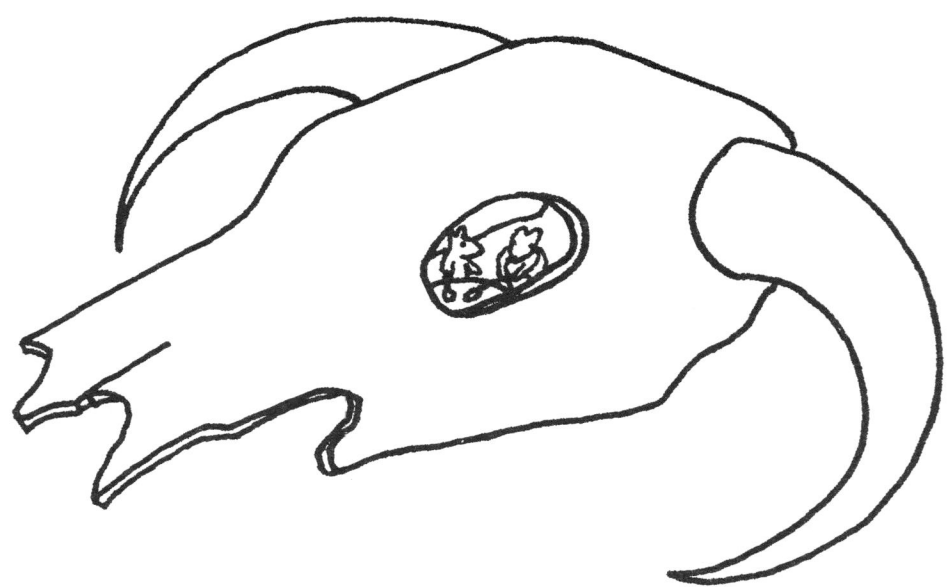

The Trickster and the Mice
A Stoney Legend

One day îktomni (the Trickster) was walking along in the forest when he heard the sounds of a pow-wow. Someone was playing drums and singing songs and having a real celebration. The Trickster wanted to join the party, but he could not figure out where the music was coming from.

The Trickster stopped to listen. After a while it became clear to him that the music was coming from a buffalo skull lying on the ground, not far from his feet. He could hardly believe his ears, but he stooped to peek inside the skull. To his amazement, he saw dozens of mice having a pow-wow. Some of them were drumming and others were singing and dancing.

Intrigued by the sight, the Trickster asked the mice if he could observe the celebration, and after some negotiation he stuck his head inside the skull to enjoy the festivities. As the pow-wow progressed to the wee hours of the morning the Trickster fell asleep. When he woke up he discovered the mice had shorn the hair from his head; then, they had disappeared. On top of that, he found that his head was now stuck in the buffalo skull.

Although he was not amused by the incident, there was little the Trickster could do about it. After struggling for a while he finally gave up, staggered to his feet and tried to walk. With the buffalo skull still stuck on his head, he obviously could not see where he was going, and soon he fell over an embankment and hit his head on a rock. Fortunately for the Trickster, the skull shattered.

Now he could see again, so he cleaned himself up and continued on to his next adventure.

12 *Legends of the Elders*

The Trickster and the Rock
A Blackfoot Legend

One day as the Trickster (Napi) was walking along, he came upon a huge rock. He spoke to the rock, "Greetings, O Rock. Here I have a fine robe that I will give you so that you may be warm." The rock was very pleased with the gift and after accepting it, thanked Napi.

Napi continued walking and noticed that it was going to rain. He told a fox who was nearby to go back to the rock and borrow the robe from the rock. When the fox approached the rock for the loan of the robe, the rock refused. He told the fox that a gift could never be taken back and he would not release the robe.

The fox came back to Napi and told him what the rock had said. Napi was very upset and decided to go and retrieve the robe himself.

Napi returned to the rock, grabbed the robe and walked away with the fox. Suddenly the two heard a rumbling noise, and the fox turned around to see the large rock rolling quickly towards them.

He warned Napi that the rock was coming and the two of them began running. The fox jumped into a hole and the rock rolled on top of the hole, trapping the fox. Napi, however, continued running.

When it looked as though the danger had passed, the Trickster stopped running and began to walk. He started thinking of a plan to help his friend the fox, who was trapped by the rock. Then he spied some hawks flying overhead and he asked them for help.

He asked the hawks to attack the rock so it would move off the hole where the fox was trapped. The hawks agreed and flew at the rock with gusto. They hit the rock so many times that it began to roll, leaving a trail of rock chips behind. Soon the fox got out of the hole and ran away.

Napi continued northward and the last pieces of that rock stopped at a spot call Rock River near Okotoks, Alberta, where some of its larger pieces can be seen to this day.

Napi and the Fruit
A Blackfoot Legend

One day the Trickster (Napi) was walking along a river bank looking for food. He was quite hungry and he was quickly growing impatient because there was no food to be found anywhere. Then his eye caught on some bright objects that appeared to be lying on the bottom of the river bed in deep water.

"Aha," exclaimed Napi. "Someone has left his food in the river and now it is all mine!"

He dove quickly into the deep water and swam down as far as his breath would allow. He came up puffing, gasping for air, but he had not reached the treasured food. He tried, again, but to no avail. Then, in desperation, he tied rocks to his feet so he could sink deeper into the water. Still he could not reach that food. When he reached the surface he thought his lungs would burst, but he still could not reach the desired fruit.

By now Napi was angry and frustrated and he decided to make a desperate move. He tied rocks to his feet and to his waist in an effort to sink even deeper into the water. This time he reached the bottom of the river bed but there was no fruit to be found.

When Napi surfaced on the water, he was thoroughly exhausted. His face was blue from the strain of the dive and he had great difficulty catching his breath. When he finally calmed down, he looked up and noticed a bunch of chokecherries hanging from a bush just before his eyes. He had been diving after a reflection in the water.

16 Legends of the Elders

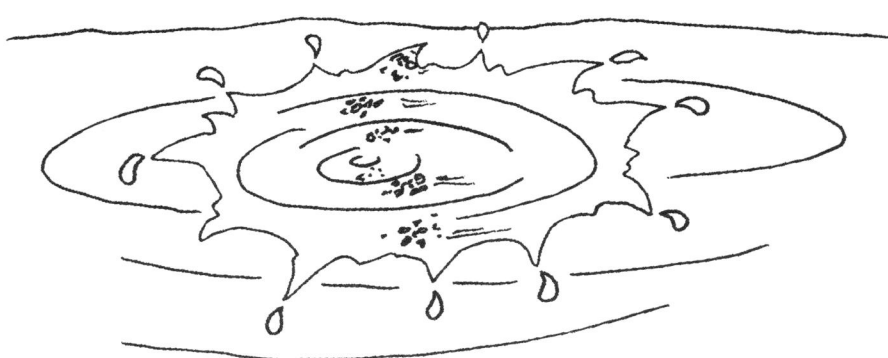

Legends of the Elders

Napi was angry that he had made such a fool of himself so he grabbed a branch and whipped the bush many times. It was a chokecherry bush. He hit the bush so hard that even today the whip scars can be seen on the bush. Today many people pick chokecherries by hitting the branch of the bush and catching the cherries in a pail as they fall.

We may learn from Napi's experience that trying to get someone else's food by greed does not always pay off.

18 *Legends of the Elders*

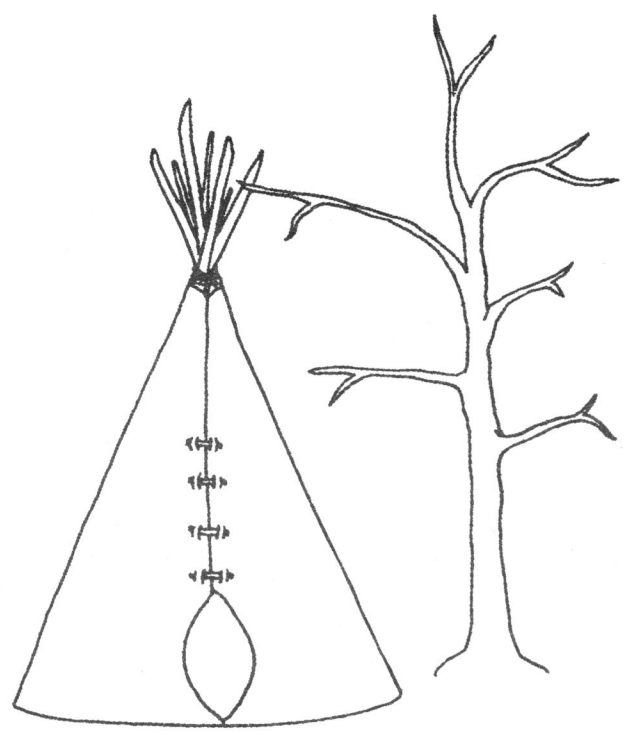

Nanabush and the Birch Tree
An Ojibway Legend

One day the Trickster (Nanabush) was tired and decided to take a nap. He entered his teepee and lay down on a nice bear rug. He planned to have a long, undisturbed nap.

He was almost asleep when he heard an eerie sound, like objects being rubbed together.

Nanabush yelled out, "Stop making that noise. This is Nanabush speaking. I am trying to have a nap. Stop that noise at once!"

The noise continued, and it seemed to Nanabush to be just a bit louder than before.

Nanabush called out again. "Stop that noise. I am trying to sleep. I am Nanabush and I am ordering you to stop at once."

Still the annoying sound prevailed, and Nanabush gave yet a third warning. "I am going to punish you severely," he called out. "You must stop that noise at once."

When the strange rubbing sound continued, an angry Nanabush got up and went outside. There he discovered the branch of a beautiful white tree rubbing on one of his teepee poles. Nanabush cut down a willow branch, and using it as a whip began to spank the white tree. He spanked it so hard that the tree got black lines all over its beautiful trunk.

Those lines remain on the white tree until this day. That is how the birch tree got its marks.

Teaching Legends

22 Legends of the Elders

Why the Crow's Feathers are Black
An Assiniboine Legend

There was once a warrior who had a wife and a young son. They were happy together, but then very suddenly one day the man's wife left their home and did not come back. The warrior was not sure where his wife had gone, but rumor had it that she had run off to live with a star in the sky. The man was very worried because his wife had told no one where she was going, and he and his son were getting very lonely. Perhaps something had happened to his wife.

It happened that a crow was the warrior's best friend, so the man told his friend what had happened. In those days all crows had white feathers.

The man asked the crow if he knew where his wife was, and the crow told him that his wife had gone to the sky with a star.

The warrior decided to go and look for his wife, and he asked the crow if he would keep his campfire going until he returned. The warrior knew his son would need the fire to cook food and to keep warm. The crow agreed to keep the fire going.

The warrior was gone a long time. When he eventually returned with his wife, he found the crow faithfully fanning the embers of the fire with his wings to keep it going. After standing in the smoke of the fire for so long, the white plumage of the crow had turned black.

To this day the crow displays his black plumage as a badge of honor and of faithfulness.

24 *Legends of the Elders*

Why the Bear has a Short Tail
An Iroquois Legend

Long ago the Bear used to have a long tail. The Bear's tail was his proudest possession and he regularly showed it off with a great deal of pride.

One day Coyote thought he should take the proud Bear down a peg or two, so he decided to play a trick on him. He cut a hole in the ice near where Bear liked to walk, and when the Bear came by and inquired as to what Coyote was doing, Coyote told him that he was ice fishing.

Bear was impressed with the large number of fish lying beside the hole in the ice, and seeing no fishing equipment, asked Coyote how he caught the fish. Coyote explained that he fished with his tail and suggested that Bear sit down at the hole and drop his tail into the water. Coyote explained that soon the fish would grab onto Bear's tail. Then Bear could pull his tail out of the water and flip the fish onto the land.

Bear stuck his tail into the water and began fishing. He asked Coyote how he would be able to tell when it was time to pull out his tail. Coyote said he would watch and when a fish had attached itself to Bear's tail, he would warn Bear with a shout. However, as Bear sat down and put his tail into the water, Coyote went away.

Night came and Bear fished on. The next morning Coyote went to see if Bear was still sitting at the hole, and sure enough, there he was. Bear had fallen asleep while waiting for Coyote to tell him when to retrieve his tail. Coyote woke Bear up. Bear was shocked when he saw his tail frozen in the ice.

"I'll get you for this," Bear roared at Coyote. Bear broke loose from the ice, leaving most of his tail back in the frozen ice. But as fast as Bear could tear his tail from the ice and start running, Coyote was even faster, and he escaped before Bear could catch him.

And that is why to this day the Bear has a short tail.

A Special Talent
A Woodland Cree Legend

Many years ago when the Cree Nation lived on an island in eastern Canada, they relied on fire to cook their food and keep them warm. One day the fire went out and no one seemed to be able to start it again. They had lost their fire. Now tribal members had to eat cold food and everyone searched for extra blankets to keep them warm at night.

One day tribal leaders held a council to decide what to do about the fire. They decided that someone should swim to the mainland and obtain fire from a neighboring tribe. A number of animals volunteered to go, and the plan was approved.

Soon it was discovered that none of the animals who agreed to undertake the journey were qualified to make the trip. Several animals like bear, fox and coyote tried, but they were not long distance swimmers. They soon grew tired and had to return to the island. The beaver was convinced that he could make the trip, since he was an excellent swimmer. However, a storm came up and washed beaver right back to shore.

Finally, the tribal elders asked members of the insect world to help and several of these tiny beings offered to help. Unfortunately, some of these small creatures drowned in their efforts to get the fire, and the tribe grew sad.

Then a water spider indicated that he would go to the mainland and bring back the fire. Everyone watched as he sped across the water, walking lightly on the water so that it seemed he hardly touched the surface.

28 Legends of the Elders

Legends of the Elders

Soon he was out of sight, and the tribe waited. After what seemed like a very long time the water spider, with his unique talent, returned with the fire. Now the tribe could again cook their food and warm their bedrolls.

After that the Woodland Cree Nation was always very grateful to the water spider.

30 Legends of the Elders

How the Ghost River got its Name
A Plains Cree Legend

Long ago, before the Europeans came to this continent, several Indian tribes were at war with one another. During one time the Assiniboine Nation was engaged in a war about territory with the Cree Nation. As it happened, a beautiful young maiden named Little White Dove fell in love with an Assiniboine warrior named Running Bear.

Running Bear was a great hero among his people, for he was a good hunter and a brave warrior. The two young lovers could not marry, however, because their people were at war.

Another difficulty for the pair was that a swift, cold river separated their two tribes, with the Assiniboines living on the south side of the river and the Crees on the north. This made it very hard for Little White Dove and Running Bear to meet. Crossing the river was a very dangerous undertaking.

One night Little White Dove's family noticed that she was missing. Warriors who were sent to search for her spied her in the river swimming towards Running Bear, who was swimming towards Little White Dove in the swift-flowing water. The river was swift and both of them were floundering badly.

The people on the banks of both sides of the river watched helplessly, because there was little they could do to help them. Little White Dove called out to Running Bear that her strength was giving out and before he could reach her, she disappeared under the swift water. Running Bear did his best to get to her but it was too late. Then he lost his strength and he drowned as well.

For a long time afterwards, at sunset in the evening when people went near the river, they could hear whispers of Little White Dove and Running Bear calling to each other.

Thus the river came to be called the Ghost River.

The Origin of Maple Sugar
An Ojibway Legend

Long ago, there lived among the Ojibway Nation a young wife who was considered to be a bit lazy and forgetful. Whenever her husband was away she took short cuts with their household duties. For example, instead of fetching water for cooking, she sometimes poured maple syrup into the stew and went off to visit with her friends. The elders were sure that someday her husband would discover her deception and they hoped she would change her ways before it was too late.

One day when the young wife was off socializing with her friends she forgot entirely about watching the supper she was cooking for her husband. Once again she had substituted maple syrup for water in the stew. However, because she forgot to stir the food, the contents of the stew-pot turned into a thickened mass and put the fire out.

Late in the evening when the husband came home from hunting, he announced that he was very hungry. He had just had a long day, but he had managed to find some meat. As he arrived home he called out, but his wife did not answer. Soon he discovered that supper was not ready, except for a blackened stew-pot on the fireless fire-pit.

In desperation the man reached his hand into the bottom of the pot in search of food and found a black sticky mess of meat. He tasted it and found that it was firm and good-tasting and very sweet. He wanted to thank his wife for the delicious treat, but she was not there, so he continued to eat.

34 *Legends of the Elders*

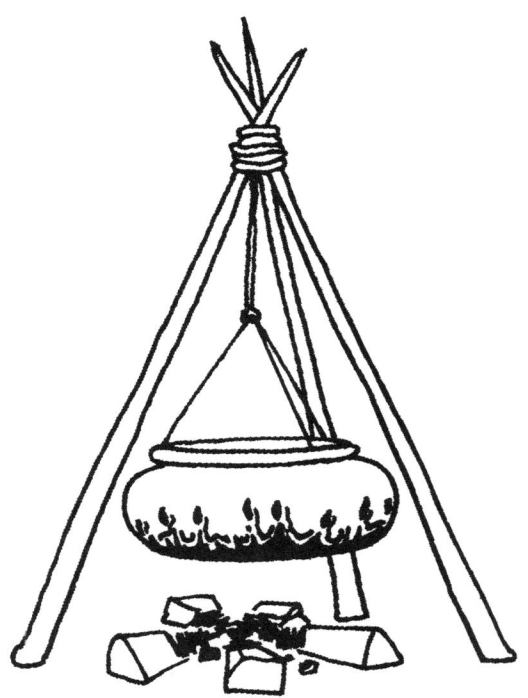

Legends of the Elders

After he finished his meal he went around the neighborhood to look for his wife. The wife was so ashamed of her negligence, she went into hiding. When her husband finally found her to thank her and compliment her for her resourcefulness, she was surprised at his enthusiasm. Her mother joined her in a spirit of shock.

"It was the most wonderful meal I have ever tasted," her husband said to her.

When she finally went home with him to taste the food for herself, she too was excited with her new recipe. The sweet substance at the bottom of the pot was indeed tasty.

It turns out that she had just, by accident, discovered the recipe for making maple sugar!

36 Legends of the Elders

The Origin of Lady Slippers
An Ojibway Legend

Long ago there was a village whose people were struck with a certain sickness. Everyone in the village was ill. Some people were so ill, they died. Even the local healer got sick and died. Now, it seemed to the people of the village that all hope was gone.

In desperation the village chiefs and council searched for a cure. They heard that in another village far away there was medicine that could help make the people better.

In those days chiefs had messengers who carried messages for the chief when they were needed. These messengers were dedicated to travel through all kinds of conditions if there was a need for them to do so.

The chief quickly summoned a messenger and asked him to go to the far away village to get some medicine. The messenger agreed, and although it was winter time and it was bitterly cold outside, he made ready to leave as soon as he could. Just as he reached the door of his teepee, the disease struck him, and he fell to the ground.

Instead of waiting for a replacement to do the job, the messenger's wife slipped out to take her husband's place. Quickly she dressed as warmly as she could, wrapping her feet in deerskin as extra coverings. Then she left to deliver the important message and obtain the necessary medicine. She ran swiftly and lightly over the snow drifts back to her village. Eventually she grew cold and weary. Finally, she stopped to rest.

The next morning the villagers were surprised to hear the woman's voice coming out of the forest. She was crying for help. When they went to look for her they found her lying in the snow, not far from the vil-

lage, unable to go any further. Her feet were swollen from the cold, but she held the needed medicines in her possession.

The villagers wrapped the woman's feet in blankets and gradually feeling returned to them. Everyone was grateful to her for having made the trip.

As the years went by the woman grew old and died peacefully. The tribe gave her a special name in honor of her devotion to her husband and to the village for her brave act.

At her death her special foot wrappings became little yellow flowers called "Way-on-ay moccasins."

These can be seen in the mountains today. We know them today as Lady's Slippers.

Moral Legends

40 Legends of the Elders

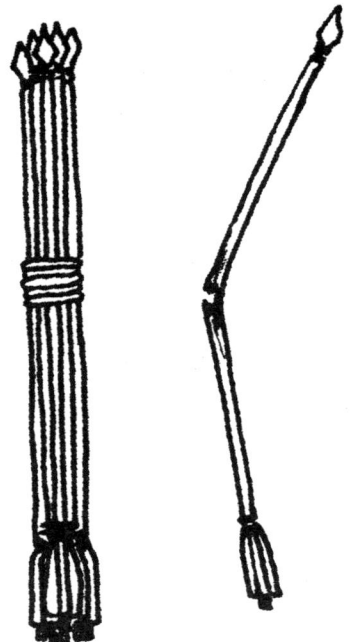

Legends of the Elders

Strength in Unity
An Ottawa Legend

When the European fur traders and explorers arrived in North America, there were many things they learned from the First Nations. They learned which animals to hunt and how to make campfires and canoes. Relying on Indian guides, they also learned the best routes by which to reach certain destinations.

Sometimes the newcomers were surprised at the way First Nations did things. The newcomers had a lot to learn.

One European visitor noticed that every year the various Indian nations in the region met for a grand council. Every tribe sent representatives to attend the council. Sometimes the council met for many days and their meetings often went on far into the night.

"Why do you spend so much time in council meetings?" the visitor asked one of the elders. "Don't you waste a lot of time talking and bargaining? Couldn't that time be spent more profitably doing something else?"

"We like to agree on things," said the elder. "That way everyone is given the opportunity to be heard, and everyone knows and understands what is going on. Here," he said to the visitor. "Take this arrow and break it."

After some encouragement the visitor did as he was told. The arrow broke easily.

Then the elder passed the visitor a handful of arrows and asked the visitor to break them as well. When the visitor was unable to do so, the elder spoke, "So you see, my friend, there is strength in consensus. Unity is strong."

Piah's Eagle Friends
A Ute Legend

One warm spring day an Indian warrior decided to locate some eagle feathers which he needed to make arrows for his bow. He knew that eagle feathers would enable arrows to fly better. Soon he was off to find an eagle's nest. The warrior took his son Piah with him, because he wanted Piah to learn how to become a warrior. Warriors need to know how to fashion good bows and arrows, and one of the first steps is to have a good supply of eagle feathers on hand.

The two travelled for many days and finally came upon the ledge of a high cliff. They climbed to the top and, looking down, discovered that the nest was a long way down. Since there was no easy way down, the warrior conceived a plan by which to lower Piah down to the nest where he could retrieve some feathers.

The warrior tied a rope around Piah's chest and slowly lowered him into the eagle's nest. Inside the nest were two young eagles and several loose feathers. They had no doubt been dropped by the baby eagles' mother. Soon Piah would gather the feathers and his father would pull him up.

As the warrior was lowering Piah into the nest, the rope suddenly broke and Piah fell swiftly down into the nest beside the baby eagles. Piah was surprised, his father was shocked, and most of all the baby eagles were surprised by their sudden visitor. Piah's father did not know how to get his son out of the eagle's nest, so he told Piah that he was going home to get some help. He told Piah not to be afraid. He would be back as soon as possible.

44 *Legends of the Elders*

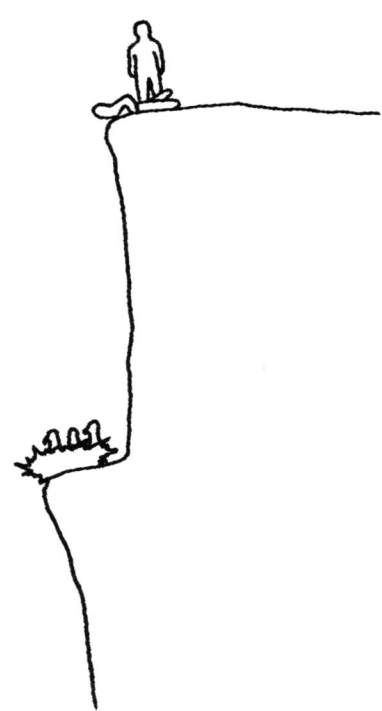

When the baby eagles' mother returned to the nest she was surprised to see Piah. She asked him what he was doing in the nest and he explained that he had fallen from the cliff above. She made him promise that he would not harm her babies and indicated that she would provide him with food during his stay. Several days went by and Piah gradually began to feel quite comfortable in the eagles' nest. He ate their food and made friends with them while patiently waiting for his father to come back.

Back at home, Piah's father held a council with his friends at the Indian village. Together they made plans to rescue Piah.

As time went on the young eagles in the nest grew big and strong. Soon they would be strong enough to fly out of the nest and soar into the sky. As Piah watched them he began to miss his family and he wished he was back at home.

One day he asked the young eagles, "When you learn to fly out of the nest, will you take me with you? I would like very much to go home." The young eagles knew Piah could not fly, and they did not want to leave him alone in the nest. They promised to take him with them when they left the nest.

Then the day came when the young birds were ready to fly out of the nest. The plan was that Piah would hold hard onto the feet of the young eagles as they flew to the ground. Then the eagles stood on the edge of the nest, flapped their wings and carried Piah safely to the ground. It was a thrilling ride, but Piah was glad when his feet touched the ground. When Piah landed on the ground the mother eagle gave him one of her tail feathers to reward him for his bravery.

As he turned to go home he saw his father coming towards him. He could not wait to tell his father what had happened. He had made some real friends.

46 Legends of the Elders

Wasted Talent
A Plains Indian Legend

There was once an Indian warrior who decided to play a trick. He climbed into an eagle's nest and stole an egg out of the nest. Then, when no one was looking, he put the eagle egg into a prairie chicken's nest which already had several eggs in it. The warrior reasoned that the mother would never know that he had added an egg to her workload.

The mother prairie chicken faithfully sat on her eggs and soon they hatched. As the chicks grew and developed, she noticed that one of them was a bit larger than the others, but it never occurred to her that one of her chicks was really a baby eagle.

When the baby eagle was grown up observers noted that he was unusually large, but he still acted just like a prairie chicken. He ate prairie chicken food, walked like a prairie chicken and flew like a prairie chicken. Since prairie chickens do not fly very high he always flew close to the ground.

One day he saw an eagle flying high in the sky, soaring over the top of a mountain. "Who is that bird?" he asked his friends.

"That is the king of birds," they said. "That is the eagle. Don't worry about it though. You will never be able to fly like that. You are a prairie chicken."

The young eagle never tried to fly like that. He always remained close to the ground, never realizing the strength that he had.

48　Legends of the Elders

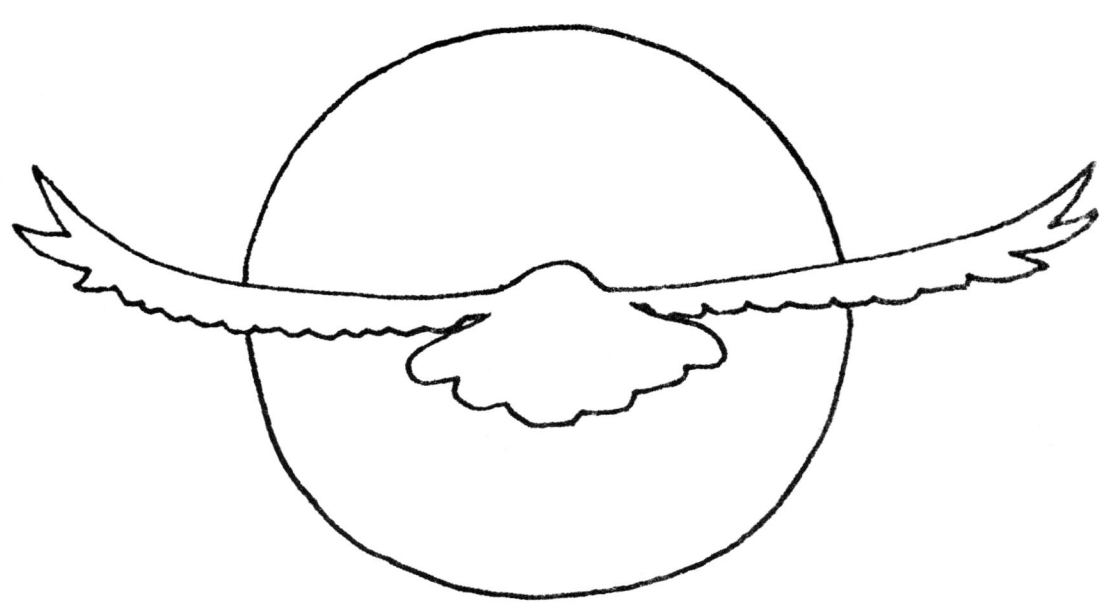

Soar Like an Eagle
A Plains Indian Legend

Once upon a time two young boys decided to put an unhatched eagle's egg into a chicken's nest along with the regular eggs. The mother hen did her duty and soon the chicks were hatched.

As the birds grew up it was an unusual sight to see a baby eagle eating in the farmyard with the chickens and other farm animals.

When the eagle was growing up, he thought he was a chicken. He obeyed the mother hen and sometimes argued with his brothers and sisters. He always won fights with his siblings because he was so much bigger than they were.

One day a man came to visit the farmer who owned the chickens. The visitor noticed the young eagle in the yard with the chickens. He was surprised that the eagle acted just like a chicken, even though it was clear that he had other talents.

With the farmer's permission, the visitor put the eagle on his arm and urged him to fly. "Fly high, O eagle," he said, "Just as you were meant to." The eagle ignored him and simply jumped back onto the ground – just like a chicken. The visitor tried several more times with the same results, then asked the farmer for a favor.

"It seems unnatural for an eagle to act like a chicken," the visitor said to the farmer. "Could I take the eagle to the mountains? That is where eagles usually live and soar," he commented. "Perhaps when he sees what life looks like from up high he will behave like an eagle."

The farmer consented and the visitor took the eagle and drove to a high mountain; he took the eagle and climbed up to a mountain peak. It was early in the morning and the sun was just rising.

The man faced the eagle straight into the sun and said, "Fly high, eagle, and become the eagle that you are!"

The eagle stared into the bright sun, looked upward into the skies, then spread his great wings and flew high into the clouds.

Now he was an eagle, powerful and free.

The Gift Exchange
An Algonquian Legend

The sun was setting in the Indian village and it would soon be night. It was a sad night for one woman because her little daughter was very sick. She had been sick a long time. When the woman's husband arrived home from a hunt, he entered his teepee to greet his wife sitting at her daughter's bedside. The warrior felt sorry for his wife, because she worked so hard to care for the little girl as well as doing her household chores. Now the little girl was finally asleep and her father did not want to awaken her.

The warrior checked the fire at the centre of the teepee and tiptoed quietly to his bed and lay down. He could see the stars through the top opening of the teepee. They were bright and shiny, and he wished they could help make his daughter well. Perhaps one day she too would shine as brightly as the stars above.

The warrior remembered the time when he was a little boy. He wanted to grow up and become a great hunter, and supply his people with food. He wanted to fight battles for his tribe and be honored for his deeds. He was proud to serve his people and he hoped his daughter would have the same opportunity.

The next morning when the warrior awoke, he found that his little daughter was still very sick. He and his wife tried to revive her strength with special medicines, and prayers were said for her by the people of the tribe.

Finally the couple talked to the elders of the tribe about their little girl. The elders said they must speak with the loon. "The loon is a messenger from the Creator," they said. "He can help you."

Later that day the warrior went to find the loon. The loon was swimming on the water nearby.

52   Legends of the Elders

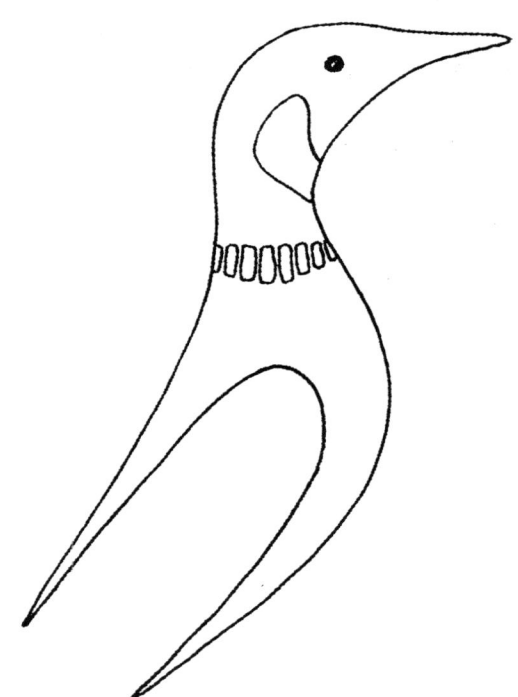

He spoke to the loon. "My little girl is sick and may be dying. I would like to ask you to help her. Will you help her?"

The loon said, "Because you have had faith in coming to me, I will reward you. I will give you a special medicine for your daughter. You must dive down deep into the river four times. On the fourth dive you will find a plant on the bottom of the river. Take it home and boil it on the fire. Make a soup, and give it to your daughter and she will get well. Now, go and do as I have told you."

The warrior did as he was told. He dived deep into the river and searched the bottom of the river. He was almost out of breath when he came to the top. He found nothing. He was disappointed; then he remembered that the loon said he must dive four times. He dived a second time, and again found nothing. On his third try he still did not see anything and began to think that he was diving at the wrong place. Still, he was desperate, so he tried a fourth time. When he reached the bottom of the river, there it was. He saw a strange-looking plant with large leaves.

Quickly the warrior swam to the edge of the river and hurried home to his wife and daughter. He stoked up the fire and threw the plant into a pot to cook. Soon the soup was ready, and he woke his daughter and gave her some soup. Her eyes opened when she ate the soup, and soon she was ready to talk. She was so happy that she felt better that she began to sing a song of joy. The warrior and his wife quickly told their friends and the tribe gathered together for a big celebration. The warrior did not forget the loon. He was very grateful to the loon and gave him a shell necklace as a gift of thanks.

"This is my gift to you," he said. "It is in return for the gift of my daughter's health."

To this day the loon wears the necklace that the warrior gave him.

54 Legends of the Elders

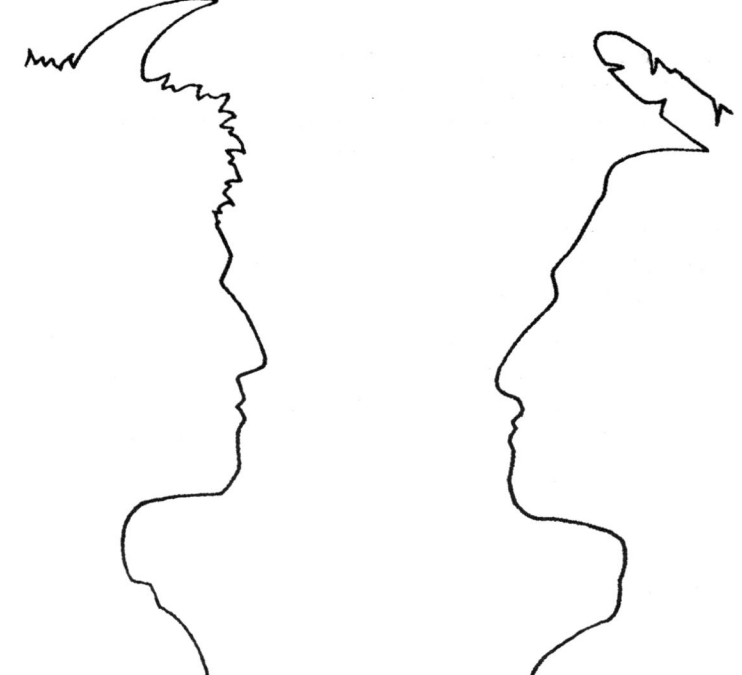

A Story About Friends
An Algonquian Legend

One of the ways that the Plains Indian people used to honor someone was to give them an eagle feather. The elders sometimes gave an eagle feather when that person had done something special for the nation. Eagle feathers were also used on arrows or to decorate a dancing costume. Warriors were always looking for good eagle feathers.

There was once an Indian warrior who went to the Rocky Mountains to look for eagle feathers. On the mountainside he found a nest of little eagles in a large tree. He climbed the tree where the nest was located, only to find that the eagles were too young and had hardly grown feathers. The man decided to go home and return when the eagles were old enough.

A month later the warrior returned to the eagle's nest. He was sure that the baby eagles would be sufficiently grown to provide him with the feathers he wanted. Since the warrior's tribe had moved, it took several days for the warrior to travel up to the nest. It was evening when he found the nest, and when he climbed up to the nest he was delighted to note that their feathers were big enough.

A sudden storm hindered the warrior from obtaining the feathers and he quickly climbed down from the tree and found a cave to wait out the storm. There was a heavy downpour of rain so the man decided to go to sleep and visit the eagle's nest the next day.

Before he entered, the warrior quickly cut down a tree branch to protect himself in case a wild animal was in the cave. It was dark in the cave and he couldn't be sure that a bear might not be lurking in the shadows. As the warrior curled up and prepared to fall asleep, there was loud thunder and bright lightning outside.

Suddenly, as the lightning flashed, the Indian saw the shadow of another man entering the cave. The visitor did not know that anyone else was in the cave. The visitor also carried a stick for protection. When the visitor saw the warrior in the cave he spoke some words of greeting which the warrior did not understand. The visitor was also an Indian and he also wore braids, but he was clearly from a different tribe who spoke a different language.

In the morning both men were reluctant to leave the cave because they did not know if they could trust one another. They tried to communicate by using Indian sign language and it soon became clear that they were both there to obtain eagle feathers.

When their meaning was clear, the men shook hands and played a hand-game they both knew. Whoever won the game would get the eagle feathers. Soon the visitor won the game and claimed the right to the feathers. The warrior motioned that they should play again. He still wanted the feathers and indicated that if the visitor won again he could have one of the warrior's braids as well as the eagle feathers.

The warrior lost again, and the visitor took a knife and cut off one of the warrior's braids. The warrior was nervous, thinking the visitor might harm him. This did not happen.

The visitor put down his knife and a gun that he carried and offered them to the warrior as a gift. The warrior put down his weapons as well and offered them to the visitor. As they traded weapons they shook hands and came to an agreement. The warrior did not get any eagle feathers and he lost his braid, but he gained a friend. Today Indian tribes still regard eagle feathers with respect and often award them to individuals as a way of honoring them.

58 Legends of the Elders

The Owl and the Goose
An Inuit Legend

There was once an owl who fell in love with a goose. Yes, strange as it may sound, the owl really *did* love the goose. His friends told him it would never work and his parents warned him about it, but he insisted. He was going to marry the goose – if she would have him.

The goose liked the owl as well, and in due course the two of them were married.

Eventually the goose laid her eggs and soon tiny goslings broke out of the eggs. They learned to walk, following their mother around. Meanwhile the owl stood around and watched.

When the goslings learned to fly, the owl flapped his wings and tried to fly along with the flock. It was hard work, but somehow the owl managed. In the fall the geese prepared to fly south for the winter. It would be a long trip.

The owl huffed and puffed as he flew south with the flock. He always lagged behind and the geese had to wait for him to catch up. Still, the mother goose loved him, and she always waited patiently.

When the geese arrived in the south they headed for a large lake. They swam out to the centre of the lake and started to catch fish. The owl imitated them and dove deep into the water.

Alas, his wings were not strong enough to bring him back up to the surface and he found himself sinking, sinking, sinking down to the bottom of the lake. There he drowned.

It doesn't always work – trying to be something you aren't.

60 Legends of the Elders

Legends of the Elders

Keeping Promises
An Ojibway Legend

One day a man was walking along in the bush when he saw a snake caught in a pile of underbrush.

"Help me," the snake cried. "I am caught in this thicket, and if I do not get out, I will starve to death. Please help me."

The man hesitated. "If I help you get loose, you will harm me. Snakes are not very kind to people. I do not want to take the risk."

"Please have mercy," the snake went on. "If you release me, I promise that I will not hurt you. I promise. In fact, I will be very grateful."

Against his better judgement, the man worked hard to free the snake. He did not want to be known as a heartless man.

As soon as the snake was free he coiled himself around the man and attacked him. The man was completely taken by surprise.

A little fox passing by heard the man's cries for help and stopped to watch. She had never seen a man and a snake fight before. She soon discovered that the man was losing the fight and he would soon die.

"I cannot help but wonder," said the fox. "What are you two fighting about?"

"The snake was caught in the underbrush and asked me to help him," said the man. "He promised if I would help him, he would do me no harm."

"No, no," said the snake. "He is the one who is trying to harm *me*. He was caught and I released *him*."

The little fox thought for a moment and then ventured, "I don't know what you mean by `caught.' Can you show me?"

Not thinking, the snake crawled back into the underbrush and was soon caught up again in the branches and thorns.

"This is how I was caught," said the snake. "I could not get out. *Now* do you see?"

"Oh, yes," said the fox. "I see perfectly. It was you who was caught, not the man."

Now the snake was very angry. He saw how he had been tricked and he did not like it. Still, he could not do anything about it, for he was caught in the brush!

The man was very grateful to the fox and offered to pay her for her help. She refused, but the man insisted. "There must be something I can do to repay you," he said. "Ask me for anything, and I will try to give it to you."

"Don't be too hasty," said the little fox. "Don't make promises you cannot keep." Still, the man insisted, pleading with the fox to take payment.

Finally the fox gave in. "Alright," she said. "There may be something you can do for me. Sometimes in the winter time, I cannot find food and I get hungry. If that happens, will you feed me?"

"Most certainly," said the man. "That is little enough payment for what you have done. You saved my life; I owe you a great deal!" Then the two went off their separate ways.

Years later the man and his family were at supper one night when they heard a noise outside. It came from the direction of the chicken house.

"Quick," the man shouted to his son, "Fetch my bow and arrows. I think there must be a fox in the henhouse."

The man ran outside, took a quick look around and saw the fox. He drew an arrow to his bow and let fly. The arrow struck its mark and the fox fell to the ground. Quickly the man ran over to make sure the villainous fox was dead.

When he reached the thief, he saw that it was the little fox that he had killed.

She raised her head for a final time and whispered her last words, "Don't make promises you cannot keep."

Then she died.